1 MONTH OF FREE READING

at
www.ForgottenBooks.com

By purchasing this book you are eligible for one month membership to ForgottenBooks.com, giving you unlimited access to our entire collection of over 1,000,000 titles via our web site and mobile apps.

To claim your free month visit: www.forgottenbooks.com/free284150

* Offer is valid for 45 days from date of purchase. Terms and conditions apply.

ISBN 978-0-656-53296-4
PIBN 10284150

This book is a reproduction of an important historical work. Forgotten Books uses state-of-the-art technology to digitally reconstruct the work, preserving the original format whilst repairing imperfections present in the aged copy. In rare cases, an imperfection in the original, such as a blemish or missing page, may be replicated in our edition. We do, however, repair the vast majority of imperfections successfully; any imperfections that remain are intentionally left to preserve the state of such historical works.

Forgotten Books is a registered trademark of FB &c Ltd.
Copyright © 2018 FB &c Ltd.
FB &c Ltd, Dalton House, 60 Windsor Avenue, London, SW19 2RR.
Company number 08720141. Registered in England and Wales.

For support please visit www.forgottenbooks.com

ADDRESS

DELIVERED AT THE

FOURTH SESSION

OF THE

American Pomological Society,

HELD IN

ROCHESTER, N. Y., SEPTEMBER 24, 25, AND 26, 1856.

BY

MARSHALL P. WILDER,

PRESIDENT OF THE SOCIETY.

BOSTON:
PRESS OF THE FRANKLIN PRINTING HOUSE,
CORNER FRANKLIN AND HAWLEY STREETS.
1856.

ADDRESS.

GENTLEMEN OF THE AMERICAN POMOLOGICAL SOCIETY:

The official position in which your suffrages have placed me, renders it my duty to address you at this time. Were I to consult my own inclination, I should listen with great pleasure to some of the distinguished cultivators whom I see around me, and whose scientific attainments and practical knowledge well qualify them for this service. But in the discharge of this trust, I am inspired with the hope that you will indulge me in the privilege of sharing in your discussions, and in the treasures of your ripe experience.

Amidst the rapid strides of the arts and sciences in our time, it is gratifying to know that Pomology has not been stationary. Few subjects exhibit so remarkably the progress of civilization and improvement as the cultivation of fruit. It is now only about a quarter of a century since the establishment of the oldest horticultural society in America. Then, these associations were few and feeble; now they are numerous and influential, extending from the British Provinces to the Gulf of Mexico, and from ocean to ocean,—all working together in harmony with each other, and aiding our association, whose field is our national domain. Then the fruit crop of the country was not deemed worthy of a place in our national statistics; now it exceeds thirty millions of dollars annually, and is rapidly becoming one of the most valuable and indispensable products of our Republic. Then the sales of fruit trees were numbered by hundreds, now by hundreds of thousands. Then choice fruit was a luxury to be found only in the palace of the opulent; now it helps to furnish the table of the humble cottager, and comparatively few are the hamlets which are without their fruit tree or grape vine.

It is only eight years since the organization of this Pomological Society; now kindred associations exist in various districts and States, and are exerting a powerful and salutary influence. Their delegates and representatives I am most happy to welcome to a participation in the privileges of this occasion.

This improvement is full of promise, and encourages us to greater perseverance. When we look back to the days of Duhamel, Miller and Forsyth, we perceive that we have made laudable progress. When we compare those numerous splendid varieties which we have obtained with the limited catalogues of the first part of the present century, we may well be proud of our actual knowledge. From the days of Henry Fourth of France, when his favorite Bon Chretien was almost the only pear; from the time of Queen Elizabeth, who sent to Holland to obtain lettuce for her royal table, down to the present century, there has been a gradual advance, but in our day it has indeed been astonishing, and still our course is onward and upward.

We have long since discarded the inferior fruits of La Quintinye, the skilful gardener of Louis the XIVth. We have few pears left of the celebrated catalogue of the Royal Garden of Versailles, and by the action of our own association we have rejected more than one hundred varieties as unworthy of perpetuation. At present, who would give a place in his garden to such pears as the Chatbrule, the Martin Sec, the Messire Jean, the Bourdon, the Lansac, the Cassolette, and a host of other worthless sorts? Some good fruits have survived, as the White Doyenne, Madeleine, Jargonelle, and others, but a part of these only are suited to general cultivation;—yet how limited their number, and how inferior their quality, when compared with our choice modern seedlings, and the royal profusion of fruits which now crown our tables!

When Van Mons, the patient and skilful observer, was successfully experimenting in Europe, our Coxe, Prince, Lowell, Dearborn, Manning, and others, had commenced their course, and obtained some good results. Then most of our pears were propagated on suckers taken from the forest; now we see millions of young vigorous trees cultivated, sold, and planted in all parts of the Union, and where twenty years since not a single specimen of the Pyrus was to be found. The public no longer ridicule the man who plants a tree with the hope of gathering its fruit with his own hands, or the saving of seeds to improve the quality of his fruits. True, Van Mons was ridiculed all his life, and only appreciated by such pioneers as Davy, Poiteau, Diel and Drapiez. His nurseries were thrice destroyed, as wild, worthless thorn bushes, under the false pretence of "public utility." This was an irreparable loss, for however much his system be discussed and distrusted, it is still true that the results of his experience have been most beneficial to the world.

An honorable member of this association and myself have in trust many of the seedlings of that great master of pomology, which have not yet fruited. We have those of the eighth generation, which, from vigor, beauty and signs of refinement, give promise of superior character, and seem to confirm his doctrine of improvement by successive reproduction. And while we are anxiously awaiting the further and ultimate results of his theory, others on this side of the Atlantic are zealously engaged in hybridization and experiments which cannot fail to be of immense advantage to the scientific and practical cultivator.

This progress should cheer us onward. No other country, in extent and variety of soil and climate, is so well adapted, or offers so great advantages to the pomologist. Not only does our correspondence from abroad testify to the truth of this statement, but our rapidly extending domain continually developes new facts in confirmation of this sentiment.

By the reports from individual fruit growers, and from associations, it appears that some varieties of the pear succeed equally as well in the extreme south part of our Union as in the north. A gentleman from Oregon Territory recently informed me that settlers there had already provided themselves with extensive orchards, and from which they gather fruits of great size and excellence. He also makes a similar report in relation to Washington Territory, and instances among others an orchard of one hundred acres, which is now yielding a large annual income to its proprietor.

A letter from the Vice President of this Society for Utah, on the borders of the Great Salt Lake, expresses the hope that it will not be long before that region shall be a successful rival of other parts of the Union in variety and excellence of its fruits. Similar accounts are received from the district of Santa Clara.

Another communication, from an officer of this Society in California, assures me of the great progress in our cause in that State, and pledges a full report of its Horticultural Exhibition for our Transactions. One of my neighbors who went to California in 1854, and now residing in Napa city, writes: "Such is the rapid growth of vegetation in that district, that apple trees, from seed planted in the spring of 1853, and budded the same year, yielded fruit in the autumn of 1855." He says, "I wish you could take a look at our peach orchard, loaded with three to four thousand baskets of fruit. You could hardly believe that the trees had made all their growth, and were most of them raised from seed, since I came to California, February 1, 1854. The crop from this orchard is now (July 18, 1856,) going to market, and we expect will amount to between ten and twenty thousand dollars." The proprietor of that crop has called on me within a few days, confirms these statements, and reports that the crop and prices fully realized all anticipations.

Such is the zeal now manifested in the cause of Pomology, and such are the facilities for intercommunication, that we are continually receiving valuable contributions from all parts of the country and the world.

When we consider the progress of the grape culture in the single State of Ohio, and its great increase in other

States, amounting now to more than two millions of dollars annually—the immense quantities of peaches and strawberries brought to our markets, the rapid multiplication of the apple, the pear, and other fruits throughout our land, and the millions of trees annually sent out from this vicinity and other parts, it is not easy to calculate the future importance of fruit culture, whether viewed as a means of furnishing luxuries for our table, or articles of domestic and foreign commerce.

In my last address, I called your attention to the importance of raising new and improved varieties from seed as the best method of increasing and preserving our supply of choice fruits. Whether the theory of the running out of varieties be true or false, so thoroughly am I convinced of the great practical utility of this recommendation, that I feel especially desirous, while I have the opportunity, of encouraging you to perseverance, and of guarding your minds against exposure to failures.

A false doctrine prevails among some, although founded on the theory of Van Mons, "*that scions taken from seedlings, and grafted into stocks, however strong and healthy, will not yield fruit earlier than it may be obtained from the mother plant.*" Adopting this theory as true, many cultivators have been discouraged on account of the length of the process. Whatever may have been the experience which called forth this theory from its learned author, in the localities where it originated, or where it has been advocated, my reading and personal observation constrain me to question its truthfulness; certainly its application to our own country. For instance, the fact is familiar to you all, that scions of the pear come into bearing, when grafted on the quince, earlier than on the pear stock. This is believed to result from the early maturity of the quince, which, while it does not change the variety of the pear, imparts its own precocity thereto. We realize a corresponding hastening to maturity when the scion is grafted into a pear tree which has also arrived at maturity; especially is this to be expected when the stock is in itself one of a precocious character. If any facts seem to oppose this doctrine, they may be regarded either as exceptions to the general law, or as the results of locality and cultivation.

The physiological principle of the vegetable kingdom under which this doctrine obtains is, that the bud contains the embryo tree, and that the strong or precocious stock constrains it to elaborate more material into wood and foliage, and thus promotes both growth and fruitfulness.

Common sense, as well as common observation, confirm this statement. Witness the pear, which we have known to fruit the fourth year from seed, when grafted on the quince. We know a seedling from the Seckel pear, grafted on the Bartlett, which bore the present season, and is only four years from the seed. The Catharine Gardette, raised by Dr. Brinckle, was brought into bearing by grafting on the quince in five years, while the original seedlings, in all these instances, are only three to five feet in height, and will require several additional years to bring them into bearing. Is it reasonable to suppose that a seedling pear, which, in two years, in a given location, attains the height of one or two feet with but few branches, will fruit as early as a scion from the same seedling, when grafted on a strong tree, which elaborates and assimilates through its abundant branches and luxuriant foliage, ten times the amount of all the elements constituting growth and maturity?

Hence, enforcing a former suggestion, in respect to raising new varieties, I respectfully urge you to continue and increase your efforts, and, in order to hasten maturity, and to multiply the chances of success, I confidently recommend the grafting of seedling fruits at the earliest possible moment.

In respect to the best method of obtaining choice varieties from seed, I urged you " to *plant the most mature and perfect seed of the most hardy and vigorous sorts.*"

Additional experience has confirmed my faith in this doctrine; for, where seeds have been obtained from cross fertilization of healthy and strong growers, the progeny has partaken of the same character; but, where the parents have been of slender habit, or slow growth, the offspring have exhibited corresponding qualities. If this fact may be relied upon, though the process of artificial impregnation be difficult and tedious, yet, pursued with skill and perseverance, it will ultimately secure a rich reward. We should not be disheartened by the poor success of Duhamel, or of Mr. Knight, with his hybridized pears; for the failure of the latter is attributable to the selection of inferior varieties, from which his seedlings were raised. In reliance upon natural fertilization, I would still encourage the continual planting of the seeds of choice varieties of all kinds of fruit, in the belief that new and valuable varieties may thus be obtained. By these various processes, we shall have continual accessions to our collections of such choice fruits as the Beurre Clairgeau, Beurre d'Anjou, and Doyenne Boussock pears. Let nothing discourage you in this most hopeful department of pomology. Go on, persevere;

> " Give new endeavors to the mystic art,
> Try every scheme, and riper views impart;
> Who knows what meed thy labors may await?
> What glorious fruits thy conquests may create?"

These are triumphs worthy of the highest ambition, conquests which leave no wound on the heart of memory, no stain on the wing of time. He who only adds one really valuable variety to our list of fruits is a public benefactor. I had rather be the man who planted that umbrageous tree, from whose bending branches future generations shall pluck the luscious fruit, when I am sleeping beneath the clods of the valley, than he who has conquered armies. I would prefer the honor of introducing the Baldwin apple, the Seckel pear, Hovey's Seedling strawberry, aye, or the Black Tartarian cherry from the Crimea, to the proudest victory which has been won upon that blood-stained soil.

But the production of new and choice varieties of fruit is not the only labor of the pomologist. The great annual loss from decay constrains me to say a word more on the *preservation of fruits*. Probably twenty-five per cent. of our summer and early autumn fruits either rot, or, to prevent loss, are forced upon the market at very low prices. In the hot season of the year, and with certain species of fruit, this evil cannot be entirely overcome; but that it may, in a great measure, be controlled by suitable fruit-rooms and other expedients; and that we may thus prolong the season of fruits beyond their usual duration, we entertain no reasonable doubt. What we especially need, is valuable late autumn and winter sorts. These, however, will not supersede the necessity of suitable storehouses, without which the heat of our warm autumnal months is liable to start the ripening process, and compel us to dispose of them.

The proper construction and management of these is, therefore, commanding the attention of pomologists, both in this country and in Europe. Their success is found to depend on a perfect control of the temperature, moisture and light. After having built and managed four fruit-rooms, upon different plans, I am of opinion that a proper equilibrium of temperature and moisture cannot ordinarily be obtained without the use of ice. The preservation of the apple is less difficult than that of most other fruits, and is tolerably well understood by our farmers. Still, how few specimens, even of this fruit, are brought to our spring market in a fresh and perfect condition! The art of keeping the pear, and fruits of delicate texture, is much more difficult; and it is to these I particularly refer.

Having heard of the great success of Mr. Schooley, of Cincinnati, Ohio, by his celebrated discovery for the preservation of meats, I opened a correspondence with him with respect to the application of the same process to the preservation of fruits. He subsequently visited me at Boston, and advised as to the construction of a fruit-room upon his principle. This I have found, during the last winter and the present summer, to operate in accordance with his statement, as illustrated by Professor Locke, in his "Monograph upon the Preservation of Organic Substances." By his plan, the temperature and moisture of the fruit-room, and consequently the ripening of the fruit, may be perfectly controlled. One gentleman informs me that he kept strawberries in a fruit-room constructed on this plan from June 1st to the 20th, in perfect condition for the table; and he entertains no doubt of its complete success in the preservation of apples and pears indefinitely. Mr. Schooley writes me that, in the month of June, he received several barrels of Bellflower apples, which had been kept for eight months, that were sold in that market, at two dollars and twenty-five cents per bushel. The remainder out of eight hundred bushels was sold at home at three dollars per bushel. These apples were purchased at random from the strolling wagons passing through the streets of Dayton, and were more or less bruised by careless picking and transportation. My own experience corresponds with these statements.

The construction of these rooms is simple. All that is required is walls made of non-conducting materials, with an apartment for the ice above the fruit-room, and with Mr. Schooley's descending flues for the cold air, so as to preserve an equable temperature and moisture, and to hold the ripening process in suspense. The air, by passing over the ice, is deprived of its moisture, and, being cold, and specifically heavier than the surrounding atmosphere, falls through his descending flues, and, by a ventilator, escapes on one side of the room, thus creating a temperature not only cool, but dry. This principle, I am informed by a distinguished member of the medical faculty, may be applied to the construction of hospitals with great advantage, so that the air may be kept at a uniform temperature and degree of humidity. For a more particular account of this process, I refer you to Professor Locke's Monograph, and to the inventor's letter herewith submitted.

In these remarks, our object has been to provide against

the maturing of fruits until the season when they are wanted for use. Care should, however, be exercised, especially with the pear, and more delicate fruits, not to reduce the temperature much below 45 degrees of Fahrenheit, lest the vital principle of the fruit be destroyed, and the flavor lost.

Time admonishes me to be brief, but I cannot refrain from alluding to *the appropriate location, soil and treatment of fruit trees.* These are subjects surrounded with mystery, and which can be relieved only by study and personal experience. The importance of thorough draining, and perfect preparation of the soil, have not received the consideration they deserve; especially where its silicious character does not furnish a ready natural conductor to superfluous moisture. Thorough draining lies at the foundation of all successful cultivation. In cold, wet, undrained grounds, the disease of trees commences at the root, which absorbs injurious substances, and the tree ceases properly to elaborate its nutritious matter. Wherever there is an excess of water, and consequently too low a temperature, and the soil is not properly drained and thoroughly worked, the vital energies of the plant are soon impaired, and its functions deranged. I am inclined to think that death by drowning is quite as common in the vegetable as in the animal kingdom, with this difference, that it is not so sudden. How many of the diseases, such as the spotting of the leaf and fruit, the cancer, fungi and decomposition of the bark, are attributable to this cause, it is not easy to determine. Perfect drainage, which should always be accompanied with subsoiling or trenching, permits the air and light to penetrate and sweeten the soil, warms it, and prepares its latent fertilizing properties for the nourishment of the plant.

A writer in the Journal of the Royal Agricultural Society of England says: "I have frequently found the soil of a *well-drained* field higher in temperature from 10 to 15 degrees than that of another field, not so drained, though in every other respect the soils were similar." Another advantage is, that vegetation seldom or never suffers from the drought, where the soil has been properly drained and worked.

The necessity of thorough drainage and perfect pulverization of the soil, is not less for fruits in open cultivation, than for the grape under glass, where one of the pre-requisites has ever been the perfect drainage of the border.

In relation to locality, some succeed best in one place, while others flourish well in several districts, and are elsewhere nearly worthless, and a few are adapted to general cultivation.

The affinity of the stock to the graft, is of immense importance to the happy union and success of both. Some unite as though ordained by Heaven to be joined, while others resist all the appliances of art. We have seen trees made sick by the insertion of an uncongenial scion, and finally destroyed. Well does a writer remark, that "it is from the analogy of the stock and graft that healthy vigor results, and unless this analogy is sufficiently close, it is impossible to obtain fruits in perfection. Not only does this influence manifest itself in the vigor and hardiness of the tree, but also in the quality of the fruit and the time of ripening." We must, therefore, learn on what kind of stock, in what soil and aspect, and with what treatment each variety will flourish best. As I have before remarked, every tree, plant and herb, from the cedar of Lebanon to the flag of the Nile, from the loftiest oak of the forest to the humblest daisy of the meadow, from the fantastic parasite luxuriating in solstitial air to the little flower that peeps from Alpine snows, every thing endowed with vegetable life, requires its own peculiar element and treatment to sustain its vigor, and secure its highest possible perfection. However varied this sustenance may be, and whether derived from earth, air or water, if it be uncongenial, deterioration and decay are inevitable. Every branch, twig and bud, every leaf that flutters in the breeze, is an organized and living body. Each has its correlative part, and any injury done to the one will be felt in the other.

Under these general laws, each variety requires a particular treatment, and should be nurtured with a wise reference to its peculiarities and habits. I am inclined to believe that the most valuable treatise on pomology would be one descriptive of the wants of each sort. The pomologist must, therefore, study the constitution and natural tendencies of each variety, as a father would those of his children :—

> "Each tree a child, your aid their weakness rears,
> Directs their youth, and tends their drooping years,
> Their different bents you mark with studious eye,
> Their laws you give, their manners you supply;
> Directing thus their flowrets, fruits and leaves,
> Your potent hand Creation's work achieves."

My experience has so often been solicited by private communication in relation to *the pear upon the quince stock*, that I deem it proper to introduce it in this connection, with the reasons on which it is founded. Many varieties of the pear thus grafted grow vigorously, and bear abundantly. I am aware that an impression has prevailed in the minds of some unfavorable to the cultivation of the pear on the quince stock, an impression which must have arisen from an injudicious selection of varieties, or improper cultivation. In this opinion, I am happy to know that I am sustained by Mr. Barry, in his address before the North Western Association of Fruit Growers in Iowa, and by other distinguished pomologists. Pears upon the quince should be planted in a luxuriant deep soil, and be abundantly supplied with nutriment and good cultivation. They should always be planted deep enough to cover the place where they were grafted, so that the point of junction may be three or four inches below the surface. The pear will then frequently form roots independently of the quince, and thus we combine in the tree, both early fruiting from the quince, and the strength and longevity of the pear stock. For instance, of trees of the same variety, standing side by side in my own grounds for ten years, and enjoying the same treatment, those on the quince stock have attained a larger size, and have borne for seven years abundant crops, while those upon the pear stock have scarcely yielded a fruit. We have, also, others on the quince, which twenty-five years since were obtained at the nursery of Mr. Parmenter, where now is the most populous part of the city of Brooklyn, N. Y., and which have borne good crops for more than twenty years, and are still productive and healthy.

That the introduction and cultivation of the pear upon the quince has been a great blessing, I entertain no doubt, especially in gardens, and in the suburbs of large towns and cities. And as to its adaptation to the orchard, I see no reason why it should not succeed well, if the soil, selection and cultivation be appropriate. A gentleman in the eastern part of Massachusetts planted in the years 1848 and '49 as many dwarf pear trees as he could set on an acre of land at the distance of eight by twelve feet, and between these rows he planted quince bushes. In the fifth year from planting he gathered one hundred and twenty bushels of pears, and sixty bushels of quinces. Of the former he sold seventy bushels at five to six dollars per bushel, and he now informs me that he has lost only three per cent. of the original trees, and that the remainder are in healthful condition.

GENTLEMEN OF THE SOCIETY:—

These suggestions relative to the progress of pomology, and the means of its additional advancement, together with the motives to future improvement, present a cheering prospect to American fruit-growers. Wonders have been achieved by private enterprise; but still greater wonders are to be realized from associated effort. How great the advantages which have resulted to our country from the action of pomological societies, especially from their lists of fruits! Look, for example, to that prepared by this society. Who can estimate the amount of labor and treasure already saved to nurserymen and fruit-growers, by its list of rejected varieties, by preventing the purchase and cultivation of worthless sorts! Its other lists are equally useful. It should therefore be one great object of these biennial meetings, to revise and perfect the Society's Catalogue of Fruits, and to render it as reliable as possible, that it may embody and transmit to posterity the ripest experience of the present generation, and become a standard in pomology with those who shall come after us.

I anticipate that, at no remote period, we shall feel the necessity of a National Pomological Institute, with an Experimental Garden, where all the varieties true to name may be obtained, where all sorts may be thoroughly tested, and distributed to the members of the society, and thus relieve the pioneers in American pomology from large expenditures and much personal inconvenience.

But I must not trespass further upon your indulgence. Yet I should not do justice to my own sense of propriety did I not signify to you my earnest desire to be relieved from the responsibilities devolving upon me as your presiding officer. These, by the aid of your fraternal counsel and cooperation, I have cheerfully sustained for six years, yielding my own convenience to your expressed wishes. I beg, however, to assure you that, whatever may be my future relation to you, it will ever be my endeavor to promote your individual happiness, and the welfare of this association.

Gentlemen of Rochester and Vicinity:—

We have come up here not merely to gratify our curiosity, or to share your hospitality, but to witness your improvement, and to be instructed by your experience. How astonishing your progress! Within the recollection of some who now hear me, this thriving city had scarcely a beginning. The surrounding territory was then what we of New England regarded as the Great West, which has since journeyed on, and is stayed only by the rolling waters of the Pacific. From a reliable source, I learn that the first nursery in this vicinity was begun in the year 1833. As late as 1840, there were only two small nurseries in Rochester, of about ten acres each, with here and there a few patches of apple trees in other parts of the country. Now pomology is here gathering some of her choicest fruits, and witnessing some of her most extensive operations.

It is estimated that, in the nurseries of Munroe county, there are thirty millions of trees, and that, in the whole of the nurseries of western New York, commencing at Onondaga county, there cannot be less than fifty millions, beside the great number which have already been sent out to adorn your valleys and crown your hill-tops. These are the precious fruits which have been gathered in this locality. Add to them the progress of this science in various other sections of our Union, and what a charming prospect does our fair land present!

FELLOW ASSOCIATES:

In view of this auspicious progress, let us compare our experience and results; let us stimulate each other to still greater exertions for the advancement of our common cause. Let us endeavor to disseminate the knowledge of the few among the many, that we may improve the public taste, add to the wealth of our republic, and confer on our countrymen the blessings of our favorite art. Thus shall we make other men happy, and keep them so,—render our own homes the abodes of comfort and contentment, and hasten the time when the garden shall feel no blight, the fruitful field laugh with abundance, and rivers of gladness water the earth.

Lightning Source UK Ltd.
Milton Keynes UK
UKHW020757270219
338009UK00008B/1762/P